GERMAN REMOTE-CONTROL TANK UNITS 1943-1945

Markus Jaugitz

translated from the German by David Johnston

An early model heavy explosive charge carrier of the 313th (Fkl) Panzer Company in spring 1943.

Schiffer Military/Aviation History
Atglen, PA

MW01487033

FOREWORD

The first volume of this series, *The German Remote-Control Tank Units 1940-1943*, described the history of these special units and the technical developments in the field of remote-control vehicles. In this the second volume, the author deals with the continuation of the Borgward B-IV series and the NSU Springer together with a number of specialized designs.

In spite of the strict ban against photographing radio-controlled vehicles, which remained in effect until the end of the war, the units nevertheless often succeeded in photograph-ing "their tanks." Most of these photos were taken in haste, so that lack of clarity must be accepted. The author asks that this shortcoming be taken into consideration when viewing some photos, for their use was necessary in order to illustrate the full spectrum of vehicles used in service.

The author also wishes to express his gratitude for new information provided by the readership.

Markus Jaugitz

"Springer" O-Series (pre-production) vehicle "No. 8" during trials in the NSU Firm's testing grounds.

PHOTO SOURCES

Fritz Trenkle Archive
NSU Archive
US Army Archive
Lock, Hopf, Höland and Susenbeth Archives
Author's archive
SdKfz 301 Technical Description and Operating Instructions

BIBLIOGRAPHY

Author's archive
Bundesarchiv Militärarchiv Freiburg
Bovington Tank Museum, Great Britain
National Archives, USA

Deutsche Dienststelle (WAST), Berlin
Missing Persons Tracing Service of the German Red Cross
Army Service Manuals
Private diaries of former members of the remote-control units

Translated from the German by David Johnston.

Copyright © 1996 by Schiffer Publishing, Ltd.

All rights reserved. No part of this work may be reproduced or used in any forms or by any means—graphic, electronic or mechanical, including photocopying or information storage and retrieval systems—without written permission from the copyright holder.

Printed in China.
ISBN: 0-7643-0185-3

This book was originally published under the title,
Waffen Arsenal-Die Deutsche Fernlenktruppe 1943-1945
by Podzun-Pallas Verlag

We are interested in hearing from authors with book ideas on related topics.

TITLE ILLUSTRATION:

B IV Ausf. C heavy explosive charge carriers of the 302nd (Fkl) Panzer Battalion in action in Warsaw, late summer 1944.

Published by Schiffer Publishing Ltd.
77 Lower Valley Road
Atglen, PA 19310
Phone: (610) 593-1777
FAX: (610) 593-2002
Please write for a free catalog.
This book may be purchased from the publisher.
Please include $2.95 postage.
Try your bookstore first.

INTRODUCTION

During the course of the first three war years the commands of the three elements of the German Armed Forces —Army, Air Force and the Navy — recognized the need for remote-control weapons technology and gave specialized companies the task of developing equipment which could meet the general requirements.

Many of these projects never got past the drawing board stage, some were tested as prototypes, but only a very small part ever saw use in a front-line role.

The agency within the Army Ordnance Office (WaA) responsible for the development of equipment for the remote-control units of the armored forces was the Office for Development and Testing- WaffPrüf6 "Tank and Motorization Section" of the Armored Forces (IN6).

As well many of the ideas for innovations and improvements proposed by the front-line units were passed on to the 300th (Fkl) Panzer Testing and Replacement Battalion, which then tested and evaluated them at its base at Eisenach or the Berka Troop Training Grounds. It was also due to the efforts of this unit that the Borgward B IV heavy explosive charge carrier was used not just for its original purpose of "demolition tank." Attempts were made to exploit the Borgward B IV and its remote-control guidance system for other purposes, in particular its use as a television picture transmitter vehicle.

In spite of the constant state of competition between the elements of the armed forces, all parties gladly "spied on" the others. The German Navy, for example, adopted the guidance system from the heavy explosive charge carrier virtually unchanged for the guidance of demolition boats.

Members of the 300th (Fkl) Panzer Testing and Replacement Battalion also played a significant part in the development of radio guidance systems for navy demolition boats. On striking the target object the forward section of the boat, in which the explosive charge and delay fuse were housed, was blown clear. After sinking two to three meters it detonated, the resulting underwater explosion equalling that of a sea mine. An hydraulic steering system for guiding the boat was mounted on the inside of the aft bulkhead. This was activated when the pilot left the demolition boat.

ORGANIZATION AND OPERATIONS

January-April 1943
301st (Fl) Panzer Battalion renamed 301st (Fkl) Panzer Battalion. Reorganized into a panzer battalion with battalion headquarters, headquarters company, four radio-controlled tank companies and a workshop platoon using the personnel of the former 67th Panzer Battalion (III Battalion, 10th Panzer Regiment). (Fl = remote-control; Fkl = radio-controlled.)

Release of officers and radio-control specialists of the 301st (Fkl) Panzer Battalion for the formation of four independent radio-controlled tank companies (311th to 314th (Fkl) Panzer Companies).

Each radio-controlled tank company was equipped with 10 StuG III Ausf. G assault guns and 36 Borgward B IVs. The 313th (Fkl) Panzer Company was an exception. Instead of the assault guns it had ten Panzerkampfwagen III tanks of various models.

May 1943
Transfer of the 312th (Fl) Panzer Company to the Eastern Front in the area of Orel.

June 1943
Transfer of the 313th and 314th (Fkl) Panzer Companies to the Eastern Front in the area of Orel.

July 1943
Successful employment of the 312th, 313th and 314th (Fkl) Panzer Companies in the Kursk Salient in Operation Zitadelle. The 313th and 314th (Fkl) Panzer Companies were subordinated to the 656th Heavy Anti-tank Battalion and the 312th Panzer Company to the 505th Heavy Panzer Battalion.

Conversion of the 1st Company, 301st (Fkl) Panzer Battalion into the independent 315th (Fkl) Panzer Company. Transfer of the 311th (Fkl) Panzer Company to the Eastern Front. There the company was subordinated to the Tiger battalion of the Panzer-Grenadier Division *Großdeutschland*.

August-December 1943
Formation of the independent 316th (Fkl) Panzer Company. Transfer of the 312th, 313th and 314th (Fkl) Panzer Companies back to Germany (Grafenwöhr Troop Training Grounds).

At the end of 1943 all radio-controlled tank units — with the exception of the 311th (Fkl) Panzer Company — were located in Germany or in assembly areas in occupied Western Europe.

January-February 1944
The 313th and 314th (Fkl) panzer Companies gave up their tanks or assault guns and were incorporated into Tiger battalions as their 3rd (Fkl) Company. The 313th (Fkl) Panzer Company became the 3rd (Fkl) Company, 508th Panzer Battalion, and the 314th (Fkl) Panzer Company the 3rd (Fl) Company, 504th Panzer Battalion.

Transfer of the 301st (Fkl) Panzer Battalion and the 508th Heavy Panzer Battalion (with the 3rd (Fkl) Panzer Company)

Vehicles of the 316th (Fkl) Panzer Company in formation, autumn 1943. As per Table of Organization 1711 f, the unit was equipped with the Sturmgeschütz III Ausf. G.

to Italy. It saw action in Italy the area of the Allied beachhead at Anzio/Nettuno.

The 316th (Fkl) Panzer Company was subordinated to the Panzer-Lehr Division as a heavy radio-control tank company and became the first German unit to receive the Panzerkampfwagen VI Tiger II.

March-April 1944

Transfer of the 301st (Fkl) Panzer Battalion back to France. There the 312th (Fkl) Panzer Company was integrated into the battalion as its new 1st Company.

May-June 1944

Transfer of the 504th Heavy Panzer Battalion (with 3rd (Fkl) Company) to Italy and action in the area north of the "Albert Line."

One day before the invasion of Normandy the 301st (Fkl) Panzer Battalion — less 4th Company — was transferred to the Eastern Front and deployed in the Lvov (Lemberg) area.

The 315th and 316th (Fkl) Panzer Companies, as well as 4th Company, 301st (Fkl) Panzer Battalion, were used with success against the Allied invasion forces. However, all three companies suffered heavy losses in the process.
Formation of the 317th (Fkl) Panzer Company.
At the end of June came the order to form the 302nd (Fkl) Panzer Battalion using three independent radio-control tank companies. The 315th (Fkl) Panzer Company became 2nd Company, 302nd (Fkl) Panzer Battalion, the 316th (Fkl) Panzer Company became 1st Company, 302nd (Fkl) Panzer Battalion, and the 317th (Fkl) Panzer Company became 3rd

Company, 302nd (Fkl) Panzer Battalion. Battalion headquarters, headquarters company and workshop platoons were new formations.

August-September 1944

Transfer of the 302nd (Fkl) Panzer Battalion to Poland and action in warsaw. The 311th (Fkl) Panzer Company was incorporated into the 30nd (Fkl) Panzer Battalion as its 4th Company.

Transfer of the 301st (Fkl) Panzer Battalion back to Germany to the Grafenwöhr Troop Training Grounds. There it was equipped with 31 Tiger I tanks. The unit was renamed the 301st (Tiger/Fkl) Panzer Battalion.

Formation of the independent 319th (Fkl) Panzer Company and deployment to the Western Front. There it took part in actions in the Liége-Aachen area.

October-December 1944

Action by the 302nd (Fkl) Panzer Battalion in the East Prussian frontier region and subsequent rest and refit at the Mielau Troop Training Grounds.

Action by the 301st (Tiger/Fkl) Panzer Battalion with subordinated 319th (Fkl) Panzer Company on the Ruhr front.

January-March 1945

Return to action by 302nd (Fkl) Panzer Battalion in East Prussia with very heavy losses. By the end of January the unit had largely been reduced to the infantry role. Part of the unit was evacuated across the Baltic to Germany.

The 3rd Company of the 508th Panzer Battalion was the first Tiger unit to equipped with explosive charge carriers in addition to its conventional tanks. Here part of the unit is undergoing training at the Mailly le Camp Troop Training Grounds.

Maintenance work on a Sturmgeschütz III Ausf. G of the 302nd (Fkl) Panzer Battalion in a workshop in Warsaw. Late summer 1944.

At the beginning of January the 4th Company, 301st (Fkl) Panzer Battalion, 4th Company, 302nd (Fkl) Panzer Battalion and the 319th (Fkl) Panzer Company were brought together at the Grafenwöhr Troop Training Grounds, where all assault guns and explosive charge carriers were turned in. The 303rd (Fkl) Panzer Battalion was formed from the three companies. The (Fkl) designation was retained even though the battalion received no radio-controlled vehicles!

Formation of a 303rd Fl-Panzer Platoon with Sturmgeschütz III assault guns and Borgward B IV explosive charge carriers. The platoon was subordinated to the 25th Panzer-Grenadier Division.

April-May 1945
Formation of the 1st Tank-Destroyer Battalion at the Grafenwöhr Troop Training Grounds. There 56 Borgward B IVs were each equipped with six 88-mm *Raketenpanzerbüchse* 54 (*Panzerschreck*) bazooka-type anti-tank weapons. The unit was subsequently deployed in the Berlin metropolitan area.

The 303rd (Fkl) Panzer Battalion and the 303rd Fkl-Panzer Platoon were committed on the Oder Front (Stettin, Wriezen, Seelow) and suffered extremely heavy losses.

The 301st (Tiger/Fkl) Panzer Battalion fought to the end in the Ruhr and was captured in the Ruhr Pocket.

Elements of the 300th (Fkl) Panzer Testing and Replacement Battalion were committed in the Fulda area without radio-controlled equipment.

The 1st Tank-Destroyer Battalion and the 303rd (Fkl) Panzer Battalion, which had by then been incorporated into the 18th Panzer-Grenadier Division, were destroyed in the final battle for Berlin.

2 May 1945. Two knocked-out Borgward B IVs equipped with 88-mm bazooka type anti-tank weapons lie amid the rubble of berlin not far from the Brandenburg Gate.

BORGWARD B IV AUSF. A
HEAVY EXPLOSIVE CHARGE CARRIER

The transfer back to Germany of all radio-controlled tank units, which was completed by February 1943, also saw the return of the heavy explosive charge carriers still on strength with the combat companies.

The vehicles underwent a rigorous inspection at the new base at Eisenach and B IVs no longer fit for front-line use were handed over to the replacement battalion for driver and other training.

The remaining vehicles were the subject of several significant modifications. Each was fitted with a three-part, folding shield for the driver made of 8-mm armor plate.

Since the 5-mm-thick hull side walls offered little protection, additional 8-mm plates were welded into place. Some of the older A-models were retrofitted with the new non-lubricated tracks as well as the associated drive sprockets. These modifications were carried out at the factory on all subsequent A-models delivered by Borgward until June 1943.

Above:
A whole row of modified A-version Borgward B IVs during transport to France. Some of the explosive charge carriers are still fitted with the rubber-padded tracks.

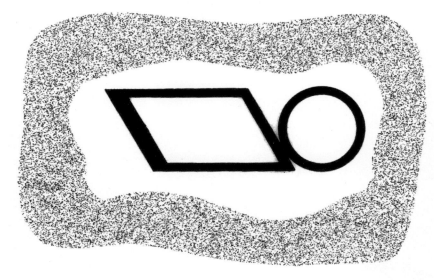

The tactical symbol of the independent 315th (Fkl) Panzer Company. For reasons of tradition — the company had a cadre of personnel from the 1st Mine-Clearance Battalion — this unit carried the rhombus with attached circle (representing the mine-clearance roller).

In addition to the new track and drive sprocket, these A-models have also been fitted with storage boxes and racks for fuel canisters ("jerry cans").

Right:
At Eisenach Station explosive charge carriers of the 313th (Fkl) Panzer Company are readied for shipment to the Eastern Front.

This B IV suffered damage to its left-side running gear as a result of driving over a mine. Here it is seen being towed to the rear by a 3-ton prime mover (SdKfz 11) of the 313th (Fkl) Panzer Company. Kursk, July 1943.

Now unmanned, an explosive charge carrier is guided forward by the control tank. The driver's armor shield is folded down. On the rear of the vehicle is the smoke generator installation.

Right:
After reaching the target line the SdKfz 301 begins laying smoke. The laying of smoke served to enable following vehicles to advance unhindered or damaged vehicles to be recovered safely.

The driver of this B IV has folded down the front panel of his armor shield in order to obtain a better field of view.

Above: Vehicles of the 300th (Fkl) Panzer Testing and Replacement Battalion at the Berka Troop Training Grounds. The soldier standing on the assault gun has hung the steering control from his belt as he uses it to guide an explosive charge carrier.

Below: Neither windshield nor folding armor screen is installed on this SdKfz 301. Note the handgrips installed on the engine cover plates; these were for driver trainees to hold on to during cross-country drives.

A section from the 2nd Company, 300th (Fkl) Panzer Testing and Replacement Battalion; Sturmgeschütz III Ausf. D with B IV Ausf. A explosive charge carriers.

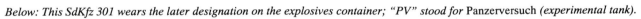

Below: This SdKfz 301 wears the later designation on the explosives container; "PV" stood for Panzerversuch *(experimental tank).*

Some of the test battalion's vehicles were powered by liquified petroleum gas. Note the two gas tanks standing to the left of this Sturmgeschütz III.

Right:
This explosive charge carrier was used to deliver rations at the Berka Troop Training Grounds, a task quite different from that for which it was designed.

The two SdKfz 301s of a training company — 2nd or 3rd Company of the 300th (Fkl) Panzer Testing and Replacement Battalion — were also powered by liquified petroleum gas.

Rear view of a B IV. Clearly visible are the rectangular openings for adjusting the idler wheels.

In addition to a large number of explosive charge carriers used for training, the 300th (Fkl) Panzer Testing and Replacement Battalion also had on strength other armored vehicles, including a PzKfw IV Ausf. G, Panthers, and various models of assault gun.

Rest break during training. Cooperation within the section was practiced in intensive training. Later in action the driver had to drive the carrier far to the front so as to make the radio-guidance procedure as short as possible.

Left:
In addition to the control tank and four explosive charge carriers, each section also had a 3-ton prime mover (SdKfz 11). It carried four additional explosive charge containers so that the returning B IVs could be rearmed immediately.

Below:
The code "114" is visible on the rear of this B IV. In contrast to the familiar company code, in this case it is a platoon designation which signifies:
1st Platoon/1st Section/4th explosive charge carrier.

BORGWARD B IV AUSF. B HEAVY EXPLOSIVE CHARGE CARRIER

Borgward began production of the B-Model of the heavy explosive charge carrier in July 1943. Three features distinguished it from the modified A-Model:

—The thickness of the armor plates of the hull side walls was increased from 5 to 10 mm. In addition to this the vehicles were fitted with 8-mm supplementary armor.

—An emergency escape hatch was installed on the right side of the vehicle above the second roadwheel; held in place by two hinges, the hatch opened sideways.

—The antenna for the radio command receiver, which was located behind the driver's position, was moved forward and mounted obliquely in front of the folding driver's shield.

The increase in armor protection was accompanied by an increase in the vehicle's total weight. In spite of this the front-line units were requesting an explosive charge carrier with 20 millimeters of armor all-round. This request could not be realized in the B-Model, especially since the vehicle was already underpowered.

The Ordnance Office called for a new design and terminated production of the B-Model after five months. A total of 360 vehicles were delivered in this time, with monthly deliveries distributed as follows:

July	1943	100 units
August	1943	32 units
September	1943	60 units
October	1943	42 units
November	1943	26 units

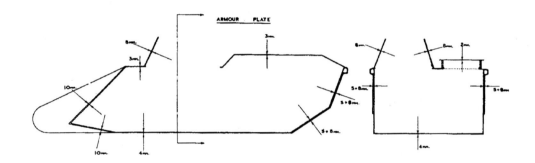

Drawings taken from an Allied report on captured German armored vehicles. The illustration above indicates the thickness of the vehicle's armor and that below the angles of the plates.

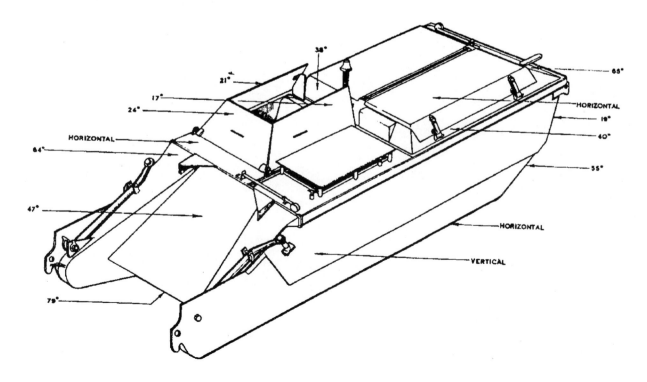

Above and below:
Heavy explosive charge carriers of the new B-version belonging to the 312th (Fkl) Panzer Company during training (above) and in service on the Eastern Front in June 1943.

A control tank (PzKfw III Ausf. M) marshals two of its B IVs into departure position in front of Kursk, July 1943.

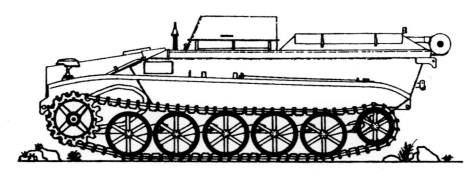

Borgward B IV Ausf. B heavy explosive charge carrier.

The tactical symbol of the remote-control units which came into use in 1943 is clearly visible on this control tank of the 313th (Fkl) Panzer Company. Beside the rhombus one can see the letter "F." This stood for "Fritschken", the name of the company commander.

The attack by the radio-control companies in operation Zitadelle resulted in heavy losses. Some carriers were destroyed in their departure positions or shortly after the start of the operation.

Left:
Since the minefields could not be marked and the relatively light explosive charge carriers left scarcely any tracks on the dried-out ground in front of Kursk, some of the following Ferdinands of the 656th Heavy Anti-Tank Regiment were put out of action when they drove into Russian minefields.

This tactical symbol was introduced by the remote-control units in 1943. The large rhombus symbolized the control tank, the inner solid one the explosive charge carriers under its command. This symbol was used by all radio-control companies and battalions with the lone exception of the 315th (Fkl) Panzer Company.

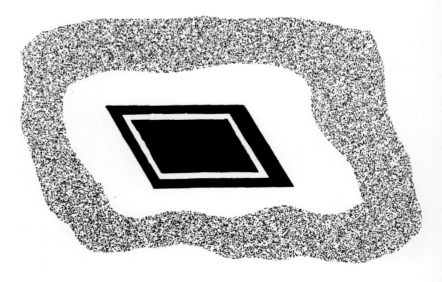

A Ferdinand passes an explosive charge carrier stuck in the Russian trench system. Visible in addition to the remote-control rhombus are the letters "Br", an abbreviation for the name of the commander of the 314th (Fkl) Panzer Company, Braam.

Two more SdKfz 301s stuck in the Russian trench system. The letters "NW" and "RW" were applied to these vehicles in chalk. This was a code which indicated the frequency range which had to be selected on the control tank's radio command transmitter in order to guide the B IVs independently.

Above: The mining of the Kursk battlefield was a serious problem. Here assault gun "02" of the 314th (Fkl) Panzer Company has sustained damage to its running gear. Clearly visible is the radio-guidance antenna mounted on the roof of the forward superstructure.

Below: This B IV was destroyed by an exploding mine, which killed the driver.

The driver of an explosive charge carrier in his SdKfz 301. Note the arrangement of the hinges on the folding armor shield.

Two explosive charge carriers of the 315th (Fkl) Panzer Company during the unit's move to France, summer 1943. In front is an example of the latest B-model, behind it an older A-model carrier.

The 508th Panzer Battalion was the first Tiger unit to be equipped with radio-control tanks (3./s.Pz.Abt. 508). A mount with the radio guidance antenna was installed on the right side of the Tiger's turret. This conversion was carried out at the unit level.

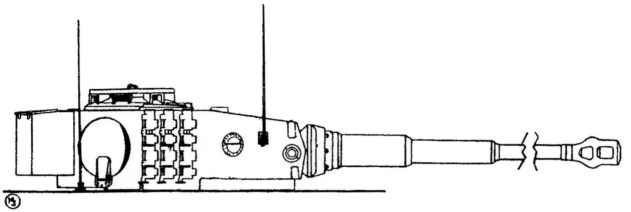

Radio guidance antenna mount on the Tiger turret.

Officers of the 508th Panzer Battalion are briefed on the operation of the explosive charge carrier. The commanders of the 504th and 508th Panzer Battalions were not happy to see their 3rd Companies equipped with remote-control tanks, as the remote-guidance procedure severely limited the Tigers' use in their conventional role as battle tanks.

22

Two Borgward B IVs, followed by a 3-ton prime mover, in the Italian theater, spring 1944.

Clearly visible on this B-model is the driver's open emergency escape hatch.

Maintenance work on heavy explosive charge carriers. The entire engine cover was removed for better access to the various drive components.

Several B IVs of the 508th Panzer Battalion equipped with removable smoke candle dischargers. Italy, spring 1944.

A Tiger control tank and an explosive charge carrier of the 3rd Company, 508th Panzer Battalion in Sienna, Italy. Although the B IVs were kept at a constant state of readiness, few remote-control missions were carried out there.

An explosive charge carrier waits in an ambush position for the order to go into action. These relatively lightly armored vehicles were favorite targets of the Allied air forces, which enjoyed air superiority.

In June 1944, 3rd Company of the 504th Panzer Battalion moved to Italy with the rest of the battalion, becoming the second Tiger remote-control company to be deployed in the Italian theater.

Below:
Another explosive charge carrier stands ready to support the German withdrawal. The effect of the detonation of the 450-kg explosive charge on the enemy forces was largely moral and helped delay their pursuit. In autumn 1944 both Tiger battalions were relieved of their remote-control equipment, which was sent back to Germany.

In March 1944 five PzKfw VI Tiger II tanks were assigned to the 316th (Fkl) Panzer Company, which became the first unit to receive the new variant. At that time the company was subordinated to the Panzer-Lehr Division, with which it saw action in Normandy. One noticeable feature of the unit's Tiger IIs was their large turret numbers. Tiger "11" was knocked out near Chateaudun.

Above: Tiger "02" was also put out of action in Northern France.

Below: In summer 1944 the 316th (Fkl) Panzer Company was removed from the Panzer-Lehr Division and prepared for transfer to the east, where it was to take part in the formation of the 302nd (Fkl) Panzer Battalion. In the process an entire transport train was shot up by fighter-bombers and several B IVs destroyed.

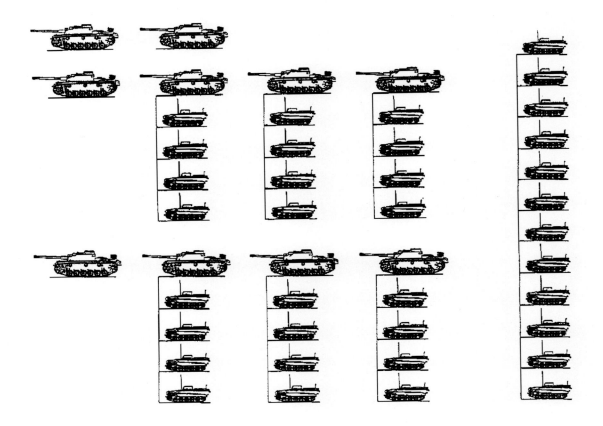

Comparison of combat echelons as specified in Table of Organization 1711 f dated 1/6/1944 "light panzer company f" and (below) Table of Organization 1176 f dated 1/2/1944 "heavy panzer company "Tiger" (Fkl)."

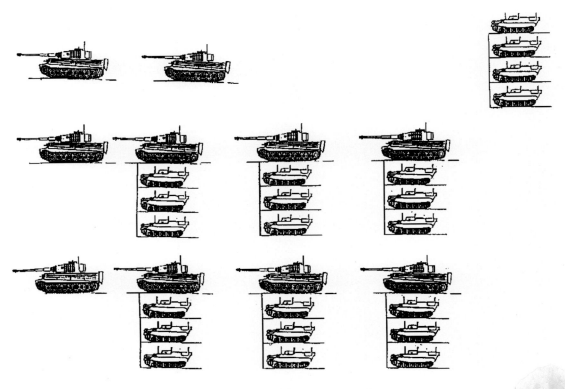

BORGWARD B IV
WITH TELEVISION CAMERA

In early 1943 the idea was born of equipping a radio-controlled heavy explosive charge carrier with a television camera in order to use it as an unmanned reconnaissance vehicle.

A "TONNE P" television camera was mounted on an A-Model Borgward B IV in an experimental installation. The control tank was fitted with a "SEEDORF P" television receiver. Both transmitter and receiver operated in the ultra-short-wave band (ca. 80 MHz.).

The Luftwaffe also carried out tests with this equipment. There the television camera was designated "TONNE A" and one application was in the Hs 293 D glider-bomb.

The 300th (Fkl) Panzer Testing and Replacement Battalion carried out extensive tests with the unmanned reconnaissance vehicle. However, results were not satisfactory, as the failure rate of the vacuum tubes and accessories in the transmitter and receiver installations was relatively high when the vehicle was operated off-road.

A B IV equipped with a television camera is shown to Hitler and representatives of the OKH at a display of new equipment (probably at Arys on 20/10/1943). Note the rear-mounted antenna for the television camera.

This modified A-model equipped with a "Tonne P" television camera was demonstrated to Inspector General of Armored Forces Guderian when he visited Eisenach on 18/3/1943.

The "Tonne P" television camera (here with outer casing removed) was developed by the Fernseh AG of Berlin in the period between 1940 and 1944. With a transmitting power of 20 Watts, the ultra-shortwave transmitter had a range of 7 kilometers in the field.

The "Seedorf P" television receiver was also developed by the Fernseh AG. All components of the transmitter and the camera were installed in the smallest possible space.

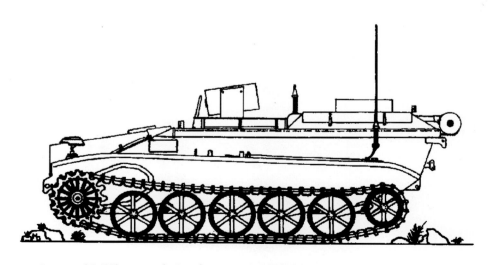

Borgward B IV heavy explosive charge carrier with "Tonne P" television camera.

BORGWARD B IV WITH FLOATS

The development of the "Ente" amphibious mine-clearance vehicle represented the firs attempt to employ a radio-controlled vehicle in the "land-water-land" role.

Since the specialized new design of an amphibious demolition tank was too costly, in 1943 a B-Model heavy explosive charge carrier was fitted with a float on each side of the vehicle. 1st Company, 300th (Fkl) Panzer Testing and Replacement Battalion conducted extensive tests with the prototype, which included sea trials in the Baltic. However, the vehicle was never used in a front-line role.

An explosive charge carrier with floats installed during trails on the Baltic Coast. No details concerning these tests have survived.

The tactical symbol of the 1st Company, 300th (Fkl) Panzer Testing and Replacement Battalion. This company was largely responsible for carrying out tests with and evaluating new developments.

BORGWARD B IV AUSF. C
HEAVY EXPLOSIVE CHARGE CARRIER

The first production vehicle of the C-version was delivered in December 1943. This new design was intended to address the wants expressed by the front-line units and the armored hull was made of 20-mm plates. Total weight increased to 4.58 tons.

The spacing between roadwheels was also increased, resulting in a more even load distribution on the running gear. The new heavy explosive charge carrier was powered by a Borgward 6-cylinder carburetor motor. The Type 6 B 3.8 engine produced 78 horsepower. In addition to the raised engine compartment, the new variant's most obvious distinguishing feature was the relocation of the driver's position to the left side of the vehicle. This made necessary a total rearrangement of the interior and the drive system located therein.

The Army Ordnance Office issued a contract for more than 1,000 Borgward B IV C vehicles, however it took delivery of only the following numbers:

December	1943	1 unit
January	1944	10 units
February	1944	6 units
March	1944	40 units
April	1944	41 units
May	1944	60 units
June	1944	23 units
July	1944	50 units
August	1944	50 units
September	1944	24 units

Difficulties with the hull first arose in July 1944 after the subcontractor — Dortmund-Hoerdener-Hüttenverein — had production problems.

Production was halted in October 1944 after 305 of the C-variant had been delivered. It is uncertain whether this was a consequence of the heavy air raids on the Borgward factory or the result of the ordnance office terminating the contract prematurely. According to the data sheets for army weapons, vehicles and equipment — Sheet G 387 — production of the C-variant was not supposed to end until December 1944.

The majority of the C-version heavy explosive charge carriers built were issued to the 301st and 302nd (Fkl) Panzer Battalions. Large numbers of this type were expended in the fighting in Warsaw in summer 1944.

Deliveries of the new C-version to the units hit their stride in March 1944. Here a vehicle of the 302nd (Fkl) Panzer Battalion.

Above: Maintenance work on an explosive charge carrier in the Warsaw preparation area.

Below: The explosives containers of this B IV are being filled with pressed ecrasite explosive. Each container held about half a ton of explosives.

Dringl.-St.:

Technische Daten:

A = 3,5
B = ~ 4   t
C = ~ 5

Gesamtgewicht des Fahrzeuges (Gefechtsgewicht)

Motor *A, B = 49 PS, C = ~78* PS

Höchstgeschwindigkeit *A,B = 38, C-40* km/Std.
Mitgeführte Kraftstoffmenge *423* l (einschl. Reservetank)
Fahrbereich mit einer Kraftstoff-Füllung:
      Straße   *212*   km; mittl. Gelände   ~ *125* km
Grabenüberschreitfähigkeit   ~ *1,34* m

Besatzung   *1 Mann   od. ferngesteuert*

Länge   *A,B = 3,65* m, *C = 4,1 m,* Breite = *A,B = 1,8* m, *C = 1,83 m*
Höhe mit Aufbau   —   *A,B = 1,185* m, *C = 1,25 m*

Bordmunition   *500 kg. Nutzlast (abwerfbar)*

Bestückung: a) Turmwaffen
               b) Bugwaffen

Abfeuerung
Optisches Gerät: a) Turmoptik
                   b) Kugeloptik
                   c) Fahreroptik
Funkgerät   *Empfänger f. Fernsteuerung (EP, mit UKE 6)*
Panzerung: Front *10mm C:20mm* Seite — *B 10 mm, C 20 mm*
           Turm ——   Dach ——

x) geschm.

					Ni	Kautschuk *Reifen u.s.w.*			
Kette *55* Glieder, Kettengewicht *261* kg *trocken 77* *300 "*									

Rohstoffbedarf	Fe	Mo	Cr	W	Mg	Sn	Cu	Al	Pb	Zn
f. 1 Stck. i. kg	*4775*				—	1	3	*17,7*	—	*7*

Preis *RM 28 000.- (B IVa)*	Durchschn. Fertigungszeit *14* Monate	Arbeitsstunden

Fertigungsfirmen:
     Montage :)
      Fahrgestell :} *Borgward, Bremen*
     Wanne : Dortm. Hoerd. Hüttenverein, Dortmund
     x) Bisher geschmierte Kette, ab letzte Lieferung B IV B u. alle B IV C Trockenkette
     B IV a u. b Serie ausgelaufen   B IVc läuft Ende Dez. aus

Sheet "G 387" in the army's data sheet series covering weapons, vehicles and equipment contained vital statistics on the SdKfz 301 series.

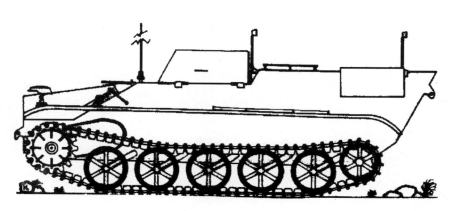

Borgward B IV Ausf. C heavy explosive charge carrier.

34

Above and below:
The explosive charge carriers and assault guns were in action almost every day during the Warsaw uprising. As a result constant maintenance and repair work on the vehicles became necessary. Anti-aircraft machine-gun mounts were mounted on the commander's cupolas to enable them to reply to fire from the upper floors of houses in the street fighting in the city.

Above and below:
These photos illustrate a remote-control action. The explosive charge carrier follows close behind the assault gun until it reaches the departure point. Then the driver switches on the remote-control system and leaves the vehicle.

The driver walks back to the escorting vehicle while his SdKfz 301 is guided toward its target by the commander of the control tank. After it has deposited its explosive charge, the carrier is brought back and rearmed.

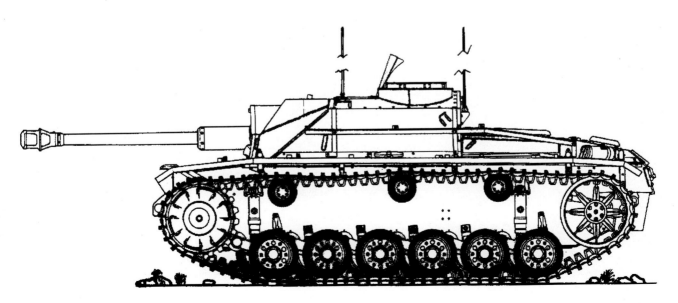

Sturmgeschütz III Ausf. G with remote-control antenna. Later vehicles were equipped with the Saukopf (sow's head) gun mantlet.

VW SCHWIMMWAGEN AS EXPLOSIVES CARRIER

The 300th (Fkl) Panzer Testing and Replacement Battalion received a number of VW Schwimmwagen, which were identical to the Type 128 but received the designation "Special Type 129."

The vehicles were modified as required for their new role as explosives carriers.

The crew compartment was completely covered with a steel plate. It was intended that the explosive charge would be placed in the rear of the interior. The exhaust system was modified; two vertically positioned mufflers were protected by rectangular fairings.

Mounted on each side of the rear of the vehicle was a sort of takeoff rocket. These were to be ignited just before reaching the shore in order to give the unmanned vehicle a push before it left the water, thus helping it get ashore.

Trials with the vehicle were extremely negative. The idea of using the VW Schwimmwagen as an amphibious explosive charge carrier was abandoned by the test battalion.

The later version of the remote-control Schwimmwagen. This vehicle is equipped with a folding windshield. The supplementary rockets are absent.

Above:
Prototype of the remote-control Schwimmwagen. A similar vehicle was totally destroyed during a test in May 1942.

Bottom:
Right:
Prototype of the radio-controlled VW Schwimmwagen, Special Type 129.

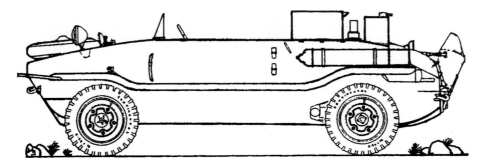

NSU SPRINGER MEDIUM EXPLOSIVE CHARGE CARRIER

After evaluating the reports concerning the employment of remote-control Kettenkrad vehicles in the Crimea in summer 1942, the Army Ordnance Office reached the conclusion that further development was warranted — in spite of the difficulties that had arisen so far.

In early 1943 the design bureau and the experimental department of the NSU Firm were instructed to begin work on a medium explosive charge carrier.

The vehicle with the suggestive name "Springer" received the SdKfz. number 304. The carrier was to transport a non-jettisonable charge weighing approximately 300 kilograms.

Like the "Goliath" light explosive charge carrier, the "Springer" would be destroyed in the explosion.

To gain further experience with the remote-guidance mechanism, several prototypes of the Kettenkrad with a special "anti-aircraft machine-gun" superstructure which were on hand at NSU were retrofitted with the radio guidance system and assigned to the 300th (Fkl) Panzer Testing and Replacement Battalion.

Meanwhile production of the "Springer" was pushed ahead by NSU, and three prototypes were ready by 1 July 1943. These vehicles retained the running gear of the Kettenkrad virtually unaltered. The number of roadwheels was increased from four to five per side, however, as a result

of which they bore a strong similarity to the prototype of the large Kettenkrad HK 102.

The driver's seat and the steering system had been moved to the rear of the vehicle, while the exhaust pipe exited the right side of the vehicle at the midway point. The muffler itself was located above the fourth roadwheel.

In a similar fashion to the Borgward B IV, the driver's compartment was equipped with a folding three-piece shield, which was intended to protect the driver against shrapnel and other projectiles. At a conference on 8 July 1943 the Inspector-General of Armored Forces requested the series production of 500 vehicles. At the same time he called for a cut in production of the heavy explosives carrier in favor of the "Springer."

Use of Kettenkrad components made the "Springer" cheaper to produce than the Borgward B IV.

The increase in weight resulted in an overloading of the standard Kettenkrad drive system, which manifested itself in problems with the transmission. This problem was supposed to be overcome by a new design.

All the necessary improvements were addressed in a preproduction (0) series. The main identifying feature was a lengthened chassis, which made necessary a larger running gear with seven roadwheels. Tests carried out by NSU revealed that the higher running gear loading caused by the

A Kettenkrad converted for radio-guidance and equipped with the special "anti-aircraft machine-gun" installation; the vehicle belonged to the 1st Company, 300th (Fkl) Panzer Testing and Replacement Battalion. At the controls is platoon commander Leutnant Haas, who later took part in tests an infrared image sensor by the test battalion.

Left: View of the driver's compartment of the modified Kettenkrad. Note the additional equipment installed for the remote-control system.

Below:
Side view of the NSU Kettenkrad HK 102 prototype. Note the forward pair of roadwheels, which were not present on the HK 101.

increase in weight placed greater stress on the rocking levers. This shortcoming was supposed to be addressed by reinforcing the lever arms.

The first 0-Series vehicle was handed over to the Army Experimental Center for Tanks and Motorization (HVPM) at Kummersdorf for testing at the end of April 1944. By July 1944 there were already three "Springers" at the HVPM, which were assigned the experimental vehicle numbers 9 to 11.

During the test phase in Kummersdorf experiments were also carried out with non-lubricated tracks. While the track maker Carl Ritscher of Hamburg developed a new track, the NSU firm delivered a modified Kettenkrad track without rubber pads. Tests with the latter proved unsuccessful, however.

Testing of the "Springer" prototypes by the HVPM and the 300th (Fkl) Panzer Testing and Replacement Battalion

continued in the subsequent months until the end of the war.

The NSU Firm began production in autumn 1944. According to Army Ordnance Office data the following numbers were delivered:

October 1944	9 units
November 1944	16 units
December 1944	10 units
January 1945	9 units
February 1945	6 units

According to information from former members of the remote-control units, some of the 50 "Springers" produced did see front-line use. So far no documentation of these actions has been found. At least two SdKfz 304s were captured by the Allies at Eisenach at war's end.

Like the HK 102 Kettenkrad, the prototype of the "Springer" had five roadwheels. Only the arrangement was changed; the HK 102 had three outer pairs of roadhweels, the "Springer" prototype only two.

0-Series (pre-production) vehicle No. 5. The running gear has again been extended by adding a pair of roadwheels. On this vehicle the track shields are absent.

This photo of the 0-Series vehicle illustrates the difference in size between man and vehicle. The forward part of the track shield is sloped; this was changed on the production vehicle.

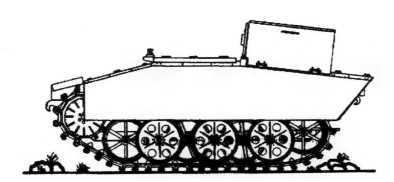

SdKfz 304 NSU "Springer" medium explosive charge carrier.

One of two "Springers" captured at Eisenach loaded aboard a rail car for shipment to England.

The same vehicle at an Allied collection point for captured enemy equipment.

A view of the medium carrier's engine compartment. All components, engine, transmission, etc., were centrally installed. The driver of the SdKfz 304 sat behind these, while the explosive charge was housed in the front of the vehicle.

BORGWARD B IV WITH 88-MM RAKETENPANZERBÜCHSE 54

In early 1945, fifty-six Borgward explosive charge carriers of various models, which had been left behind at Grafenwöhr Troop Training Grounds by remote-control units which had been converted to other roles, were modified to serve as tank-destroyers. Given the job of converting the vehicles was the workshop and ordnance shop of the 5th Panzer Replacement Battalion. The remote-guidance systems were removed from the B IVs and additional armor was installed.

As armament the vehicles were each fitted with six bazooka-type anti-tank weapons designated Raketenpanzerbüchse 54. These were mounted on a movable six-barrel launcher or in fixed mounts.

All B-IV tank-destroyers were assembled in the 1st Tank-Destroyer Battalion and saw action in the Battle of Berlin.

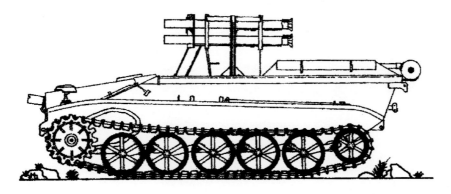

A version of the Borgward B IV with 88-mm Raketenpanzerbüchse 54 bazooka-type anti-tank weapons.

The final battle, Berlin, 1945. Various versions of the "Borgward tank-destroyer" saw action in the center of the Reich capital. There they participated in the bitter final battles between the Reichstag and the Brandenburg Gate.

BORGWARD B IV ARMORED MUNITIONS CARRIER

At the end of 1944 explosive charge carriers no longer suitable for use as remote-control vehicles were modified to serve as armored munitions carriers. Three armored munitions carrier companies were formed, each with 15 vehicles, and subordinated to the following units:

801st Armored Munitions Carrier Company 1st Infantry Division
802nd Armored Munitions Carrier Company 170th Infantry Division
803rd Armored Munitions Carrier Company 28th Light Infantry Division

Generally the employment of armored munitions carrier companies was a success.

A report by the 803rd Armored Munitions Carrier Company reveals that on 12 January 1945 ten carriers made a total of 22 trips to the division's front line and delivered 14.1 tons of small arms ammunition. After the start of the Soviet offensive in mid-January 1945 all the munitions carriers were immobilized by a lack of fuel or want of maintenance and had to be blown up.

Photographed in a German city after the war's end, a B IV Ausf. A converted to serve as an armored munitions transporter.

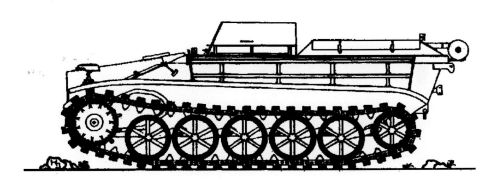

Borgward B IV as armored munitions transporter.

BORGWARD B IV WEAPONS PLATFORM

Documents from the files of the Inspector General of Armored Forces reveal that towards the end of the war there were plans to use some surplus B IVs as weapons platforms.

There are no exact figures as to the number of vehicles converted.

It is known that B IV weapons platforms did see service. Formation of the 2nd Panzer Company Kummersdorf was completed by the Army Test Center for Tanks and Motor-ization at Kummersdorf at the beginning of April 1945. The mixed reconnaissance platoon of this unit, which possessed a wide variety of equipment, had on strength one B IV Ausf. C armed with a 20-mm cannon and two B IV Ausf. C armed with machine-guns.

No further details are available concerning the use of the three weapons platforms.

Lethal danger! On the morning of 5/7/1943 an error in the ignition system set off the explosive charge of this B IV as it sat in its readiness position. The force of the explosion also destroyed the control tank and killed several members of the 313th (Fkl) Panzer Company.

EPILOGUE

Of the more than 1,000 heavy explosive charge carriers built, 318 were still on strength at the end of February 1945.

Many explosive charge carriers were destroyed by explosions in the course of the sporadic remote-control missions that still took place during the defensive battles. The majority, however, were blown up as a result of lack of fuel. At the end of January 1945 the 302nd (Fkl) Panzer Battalion was forced to destroy all of its remaining 65 B IVs for this reason on orders of the "Großdeutschland" Panzer Corps!

In the period after 1945 repaired B IVs were used as agricultural tractors in the former Soviet occupation zone.

While today many military museums are able to display "Goliath" light explosive charge carriers in their collections, the number of "surviving" medium and heavy carriers is very small.

A B-Model Borgward B IV is in the Musée Automobiles de Normandie in Cleres, France, another in the Kubinka Tank School in Russia. An NSU Springer forms part of the collection of the Bovington Tank Museum in England.